Lorikeet's Tasty Adventure
Second Edition

Rainbow Lorikeets are so full of life, their fun-loving, mischievous nature is captivating.

This story, the second in the Lorikeet's Book Series for young readers is based on a family of Lorikeets whose chicks leave the nest without letting anyone know where they are going.

Through my words and the creative vision of Lillian Falzon, whose illustrations brought these characters to life, I hope you enjoy a peek into the adventures of this quirky, colourful family.

Lawrence the Rainbow Lorikeet, his life partner
Loretta and his family are in a shady tree napping out
of the hot midday sun.

Larry (Lawrence Junior) can't sleep and looks around to
see who else is awake when he sees his sister Loren look
up at him.

Larry, who is a mischievous Lorikeet, wants to go on an adventure and asks Loren if she would like to go with him.

Loren is older than Larry but has never left the nest without her parents and is a little scared. Larry assures her that it will be okay and he will look after her.

Loren agrees to go, they both quietly leave the nest unseen and fly off to explore.

They dart up and down, in amongst branches and through the trees when they find themselves back at the garden where their father had brought them for breakfast.

Larry discovers a strange looking tree with bright green shiny leaves and interesting orange balls hanging on it.

Larry and Loren fly past and around the strange tree to have a closer look and then land in another tree nearby.

Larry flies off again and lands in the unusual tree with the orange balls and hangs upside-down, poking one with his beak.

He calls to Loren to come and have a look. Loren flies into the tree and they both poke one of the balls and try to grasp it with their claws when it drops to the ground and splits open.

Larry flies down and finds the orange ball has a delicious aroma coming from the inside.

Upon closer inspection with his beak, he discovers the outside is bitter tasting and shakes his head. He chirps at Loren to fly down and try the strange food.

Loren cautiously has a look around to see if it is safe, then flies down and hops around, inspecting the orange ball. Loren then joins Larry as he starts eating the inside.

Before long Larry and Loren have eaten the whole ball and fly back up into the tree and begin poking and chewing the outside of another of the orange balls to get inside to the delicious centre.

Larry and Loren are so busy with their new found meal, they don't hear their father Lawrence calling them.

The chicks are just getting started on the third ball when Lawrence flies by and spots the pair of them in the tree and screeches at them to return to the nest.

Larry and Loren get such a shock that they drop the orange ball and fly off immediately toward home, closely followed by Lawrence.

Back at the nest their brothers and sisters are awake and chattering, waiting for their return. Their mother Loretta is upset.

She and Lawrence take Larry and Loren aside and explain the importance of not leaving home without letting them know where they are going.

Larry tells his mum, about the amazing tree he and Loren discovered with the delicious orange balls. He tells Loretta how amazing the balls tasted and how they made his tummy gurgle.

Loretta explains that the orange balls are mandarins and that the outside skin is bitter because it is a citrus fruit and if you eat too many, they will give you a tummy ache.

Larry and Loren share their adventure with their brothers and sisters and then they all settle in the nest for the afternoon.

Lawrence tries to have a nap but keeps one eye on the mischievous pair until they are both asleep. Loretta sighs and is thankful her two youngest children are home safe.

Lorikeet's Tasty Adventure

ISBN

978-1-7640295-3-7 (Paperback)

978-1-7640295-4-4 (eBook)

www.ingramcontent.com/pod-product-compliance
Lightning Source LLC
Chambersburg PA
CBHW060842270326
41933CB00002B/169